I Can't Is For Broke Folks

Christopher C. Sands

Published In Part By:
Covenant Brothers Publishing
Huntsville, Alabama

I Can't Is For Broke Folks

DEDICATION

This book is dedicated to my niece, *Seniyah Deshay Peak.*

You were such a precious and perfect gift. I am elated to have had the opportunity to hold, spend time, and interact with a true ANGEL. As you watch over us from the heavens, know that in our hearts, we will forever cherish those moments in which you graced us with your beautiful presence. My precious Angel, R.I.H. Love you ALWAYS....

Make your donation in honor of Seniyah by visiting http://cjsids.donorpages.com/Memorial/SeniyahPeak/#sidsawareness

TABLE OF CONTENTS

PREFACE

I Can't Is for Broke Folks came to me in a dream. I was in a place where I'd given God every excuse as to why I couldn't do what He asked of me. Well, God, I am not the best speaker. I don't have the resources. I am not tall enough, fine enough. I have a past filled with failure and regret. I still sin. I... I. . . I . . . just can't do it! All of my excuses began with the word "I." The reason I didn't want to do it was not because the instruction came from God, but because of fear of what people would have said or thought.

Are you currently in this place of doubt and confusion? Does it seem as if you don't know where you are and what you should be doing? Are you giving God every excuse as to why you can't do what He has created you to do? If you have answered yes to any of these questions you are not alone. It is my desire to help you in shifting your mindset from I CAN'T to I CAN, I WILL, I MUST and I AM.

This is more than a book; this is a self-awareness guide. My prayer for you is that you allow *I Can't Is For Broke Folks* to guide you into a journey of changing your mind and ultimately changing your world. This book will shift your perspective and help you to reduce unnecessary stress in your life by focusing on what is important—a better you! At the end, you will find journaling questions to use daily as you overcome the "I Can't" mindset. Don't forget to sign your *I Can Agreement*! I'm excited about our journey together!

Let's get to it!!

<u>Chapter One</u>

THE "I CAN'T" MINDSET

To hell with the words, "I CAN'T!" These two words alone have crippled children, teens, and adults for centuries. These simple words start off innocent in nature, but over time literally change the fabric of our minds.

The words "I can't" bind us to our past experiences of failure. What provokes these "I can't" thoughts? It's simple. Fear of failure. Maybe it was the first time you rode a bike and you fell or ran for class president and you lost. Perhaps you gave someone your heart and they broke it or you attempted to start your first business and it was unsuccessful. Those moments made you afraid to try again—afraid to chase your dreams.

Those moments opened up the seams in your brain to accept "I Can't" as a reason to not even try. If you didn't properly deal with those feelings of failure THEN, they are still affecting the fabric of your mind NOW. For this reason, when we start off with "I can't" we never "DO" because we are stuck in a mindset where we are still frustrated about things that occurred in the past.

MIND FABRIC: HANDLE WITH CARE

We are all familiar with the term, fabric. It is used to define material that has been woven, knitted, or even textured for the use of creating shoes, clothing, home décor, etc. Fabric can also be described as the framework or structure that makes up an entity.

For example, the fabric of a school consists of principal(s), students, teachers, and so on. What many of us are not familiar with, however, are the similarities of fabric and our minds. Fabrics are typically put together as a working framework for something else.

Our minds work the same way as it pertains to what we think and believe we are capable of achieving. We "weave" in thoughts and ideas contingent upon what we take in from our surroundings. What we say, think, and surround ourselves with hold weight and "texturize" our hearts and minds. When we allow ourselves to take in negativity, we subconsciously "knit" in thoughts that keep us stuck wherever we may be. For these reasons, we must handle our mind fabric with care.

Think about the tags on delicate clothing. The tags give us details on the upkeep of the delicate fabric in which the clothing is made of, so that each time we wear that Versace shirt or that Michael Kors dress, it is at its absolute best.

Delicate fabrics cannot go through the same wash/dry process as other clothing, nor can it be relieved of stain as easily as other clothing. So when we wear clothing made of delicate fabric, we are more particular about the things we come in contact with—things that could potentially stain or ruin the fabric and prevent us from ever wearing that Versace shirt or Michael Kors dress again.

We must take these same precautions when dealing with our delicate minds. What inhabits the mind can hinder the mind. We must be careful of the thoughts, words, and surroundings we allow to move-in and affect the most delicate fabric we own—our minds.

WATCH YOUR S.T.E.P. (SPEECH, THOUGHTS, ENVIRONMENT, PURPOSE)

Let's think about the times and instances in which we say "I can't" on a daily basis:

I can't find my keys.

I can't meet at that time.

I can't seem to pull that up on my computer.

I can't get to that right now.

I can't open this.

I can't pay that bill.

I can't decide what I want for dinner.

I can't take that class this semester.

I can't concentrate right now.

I can't hear you.

I can't get this problem right.

I can't believe her.

Girl, I can't believe that.

I can't understand.

I can't be bothered.

The list goes on and on. So let's say, hypothetically, we say "I can't" at least 150 times a day. There are seven days in a week. At this rate, we've used the phrase "I can't" 1,050 times in one week, 4,200 times in a month, and 50,400 times in a year, roughly. Man, that's CRAZY!

Let's take it a step further. Studies show that on average, we think about 60,000 thoughts and say 20,000 words per day. This suggests that we verbalize less than 50% of what we actually think. So the 150 times daily that we verbalize "I can't" on minor, trivial matters only reflect 50% of the "I can't" thoughts we actually have in our minds. This high usage of the term "I can't" is detrimental to your purpose.

Why hold onto things that are negatively affecting your purpose? When we spring clean, we refresh our homes; we clear our homes of things we no longer use. You no longer have use for the words "I Can't". So, when will you "refresh" and "spring clean" your mind? Take it out of your vocabulary. Clean your mind of CAN'T.

If you are comfortable with using "I can't" on minor issues, it's even easier to use on major issues, like your purpose. On the following page, I have listed just a few ways that we can begin to take "I Can't" out of our daily vocabulary.

The "I Can't" Mindset says:	The "I Can" Mindset says:
I can't meet at that time.	My schedule does not allow a meeting at that time.
I can't find my keys.	I have misplaced my keys.
I can't decide on what I want to eat.	I am still deciding what I want to eat.
I can't believe he/she did that!	I am surprised that he/or she said that.
I can't understand.	I am still trying to understand.

Research shows that when we tell ourselves something a number of times, we begin to believe it. What we speak is one thing, however, what we continuously speak affects our mental make-up – our mind fabric.

For instance, a lot of people say they are not great at math, or that math isn't a strong subject for them. Let's say they began to realize and own this self-doubt around their middle school years. By the time they reach adulthood, they've spoken this doubt of mathematical success so many times that they deal with anything pertaining to math with a preconceived notion of failure. This is a form of conditioning.

> **Conditioning**[1]: the act or process of TRAINING something to act, respond, or behave a certain way in a certain situation.
>
> *Examples:*
>
> After you wash your hair, you condition it for softness and easy management when it is time to style.
>
> *Or,*
>
> When you discipline a child, you are conditioning them to associate scolding (fussing) and physical behavior correction (Belts, Switches, or HANDS depending on the parent, the problem, and what's in reach) with disobedience.

What we allow to occupy our thinking has a powerful impact on what we are and what we are to become. So when we tell ourselves "I can't", we condition our brains to associate FAILURE with our PURPOSE. Allow me to make it plain. When you are in an "I can't" state of mind, any time you even think of your purpose, your mind INSTANTLY gives it a new address.

When you tell yourself, "I can't", your mind packs your purpose into boxes labeled "DO NOT OPEN", puts those boxes on a moving truck, drives to YOUR PAST, and unpacks your purpose at the front door of FAILURE. Now, your purpose exists and resides only in FAILURE.

Know this—your purpose is everything that you are, your reason for even existing. So if your purpose exists in failure, YOU EXIST IN FAILURE. You can't be in a place of success physically if mentally you only exist in your failures.

If you want your life to flourish and prosper in your purpose, start by looking at the activity of your thought-life. Negative thoughts have the potential to place you in a corner that you never want to come out of – they box your will to succeed. Think about all the things you were truly capable of accomplishing, but didn't simply because you THOUGHT you couldn't. No effort, no attempt, just a thought was enough to stop you dead in your tracks. Let's be real. Part of you said "Let's do it!" However, there was another voice that spoke "This is not you, you can never do that."

It's amazing that in our ONE mind there are several voices that speak to us. One is a voice of fear. The other is a voice of faith. We must decide daily which voice we will listen to, which voice we will believe, and which voice we will obey.

You are a product of your thoughts; no matter what they may be. Positive thoughts produce positivity, negative thoughts produce negativity. The question is, what have you been thinking about?

KEEPING THE "SQUARES" OUT OF YOUR "CIRCLE"

Let's think of a circle from a geometric standpoint. The ends of a circle meet and create a perfect circumference. If you place a dot in the center of a circle and use a ruler to measure the distance from the dot to the outer lining of the circle, you will find that from every direction you turn the ruler, the distance from the dot to the circle's lining is exactly the same. So to place a square in a circle not only messes up the circumference of the circle, but it creates points that do not equally measure back to the center. With that being said, what are you forcing in your circle that does not align with your center focus, the core of your existence, YOUR PURPOSE?

The rap hit "Squares out Your Circle"[2] by Rocko ft. Future suggests that there are people around us who try to discourage us and hinder our successes. However, it doesn't stop there. Everything that make up our environments has the potential to throw us off track and away from our purposes. Find ways to surround yourself with people, songs, places, and things that align with your purpose and dreams. If it is your dream to own a home, find your desired home and walk around it as if you already own it. Drive by every day, park in its driveway, take off your shoes and walk through the lawn, or whatever it takes to make your dream real!

As mentioned earlier, it is very important to surround yourself with like-minded people. Friends and associates who are always sad, depressed, and negative will eventually render the same feelings within you. Find ways to redirect their negative statements, even if they are just speaking of themselves. Allow them to see the positivity brimming within you. Sometimes, you can't give mouth to mouth resuscitation to other people's purposes.

You will eventually find yourself with a breathless, lifeless purpose of your own. Stop letting people take your breath away! Before you allow your lungs to collapse trying to breath into them, remove them from your circle altogether. They didn't fit anyway! It is okay to love people from a distance— OUTSIDE of your circle. Your purpose depends on it.

OVERCOMING THE "I CAN'T" MINDSET

Do you brush your teeth with your dominate hand only? What happens if you try to use the opposite hand to complete this regular task? Try it! I'll give you a few minutes! You will find that it's not impossible to do, but it is definitely different! You may feel the same when you begin walking in your purpose with a new mindset. Remember that you are breaking the systematic way in which your mind has been conditioned to think. This is a process, and all processes take time if they are to be done correctly. The process will be different, not difficult, and not impossible.

Keep in mind that it takes about 21 days to make or break a habit. Don't expect immediate results over-night. When we walk up steps, we take them one at a time. Right? We find that each step takes us higher and higher towards our destination. Take this same approach in overcoming the "I Can't" mindset and make conscious efforts towards positive thinking, one day at a time.

Chapter Two

YOU ARE PURPOSED TO WIN

"They know the fate of the world is lying in their hands.

They know to only use their weapons for defense.

No one will ever take them down,

the power lies on their side.

Go, Go Power Rangers

Go, Go Power Rangers

Go, Go Power Rangers

You Mighty Morphin' Power Rangers

No one can ever take them down

The power lies on their side"

-Excerpt from the Mighty Morphin' Power Rangers theme song[3]

Okay. First of all, don't judge me! Second of all, don't act as though by the second line (once you recognized the lyrics) you didn't begin to sing along!

Growing up, I was a huge Power Rangers' fan. At school, I didn't think about school. I thought about getting back home to watch the Power Rangers. It's not like anything new happened. Every episode was like the one before. The Power Rangers would be at their spot or wherever. You know, just chilling. It seemed like out of nowhere, a situation would occur and the Power Rangers would have to drop whatever they were doing, suit up and save the world. I often wondered, dang, do the Power Rangers ever get a day off? I'm just saying, can there be one episode when they do absolutely nothing? No wars to fight, no evil villains to destroy, no planets to save—just chill. The answer is no.

When Saban Entertainment first produced Power Rangers, they understood that in order for the show to have purpose, there must be conflict. How else would we know that Jason (the red one…the best one) was an awesome leader, if there was never a battle in which he could lead his team?

Now check out your own life. What would it be like if there were no conflict? I don't know about you, but the thought alone freaks me out! There's an old cliché that says "Test and trials come to make us strong." I'm not sure who started that, but they left off a few things. Test and trials not only come to make us strong, but they also come to define our purpose and our reason for being alive.

YOU STILL HAVE PURPOSE

I am constantly traveling from Chattanooga, TN to Christiana, TN to be with my youth group, SWAGG (Serving with a Great God). While on the road one evening, a car sped past, jumped in front of me, and slammed on breaks. I, without hesitation, swerved close to the median. The only thing I could say was "JESUS!" I didn't say his name just to be saying it, but because my conditioning and experience with Him reminded me from where my help comes. In that moment, I realized I still have a purpose for being here.

I'm sure many of you have had near-death experiences that caused you to open your eyes and take a front row seat at the world premiere of your own life! The reason certain situations that should have destroyed you DIDN'T destroy you is because there is a purpose and a plan for your life that you must fulfill.

As we discussed in Chapter 1, our purposes are the reason we even exist. They are given to us by God, therefore we live to serve him. There is absolutely nothing that can destroy us if He still has purpose for us! Our purpose is our saving grace. If this is our saving grace, then why do we have a hard time accepting it? Like, bro, the reason you didn't get caught up in the streets is because you still have purpose. That bullet that flew pass you at the club, didn't kill you because you still have purpose. Remember those nights you were so "turnt up" you decided to drive yourself home drunk? You dodged an accident because you still have a purpose! When will you accept your "saving grace"? When will you begin to live in your purpose?

It's hard to talk about purpose without talking about Jeremiah. You see, Jeremiah was 17 when God revealed to him his purpose. Let's stop right there. Jeremiah was 17! Honestly, I cannot begin to tell you what was on my mind at 17, but it was most definitely not my purpose. The story of Jeremiah is inspiring because like many of us today, Jeremiah had a hard time seeing and accepting his purpose. I can't say that I blame the man! In my mind, I can see Jeremiah pleading with God like, "Look, God, I'm too young for all of that. My friends will look at me funny. I haven't even had the chance to "turn up" yet!"

Maybe your doubt looks different from Jeremiah's doubt. Maybe you feel like you aren't smart enough, you don't have the time or resources, or you just down-right don't feel worthy to complete your assignment. Whatever the case maybe, know this—you are the perfect fit for God's perfect will in your life. When we tell God "I can't" it is literally a slap to His face. Why is this such an insult to God? It's simple. He knows that He has instilled in us the raw materials we need to be successful and achieve greatness. When we say to Him "I can't" we suggest that the enemy (the voice of the "I can't") has greater power than God (the will by which we can).

For 40 years, Jeremiah preached the same sermon about the demise of Jerusalem and the sin of worshipping of idol gods. He did this for 40 LONG years before Jerusalem even fell. That's not even the mind-blowing part about it. Would you believe that within those 40 years, the people of Jerusalem still didn't listen? They heard the SAME sermon for 40 years and kept right on doing what they were doing. I don't know about you, but I probably would have called it quits after about the first 4 days. I'd have been like, you know what, if you all don't want to listen, that's fine. I admire the story of Jeremiah.

So often, we cease in our purpose because we feel as though we aren't making a big enough impact. Among many things, Satan is a liar! He tried Jeremiah just as he tries us today. Satan attempted to throw Jeremiah off his purpose by making him believe that his work was in vain. The devil will tell you half-truths just to impress you with full lies!

Have you ever heard of the Domino Effect? If you haven't, go to YouTube, type it in and watch how it works. The Domino

Effect occurs when one small action sets off a ripple effect of other actions. As one domino falls, it hits the domino in front of it. That domino falls, and hits the one in front of it, and so, and so on. Let's just say, one domino fails to fall upon the next. The entire effect stops.

The Domino Effect says to us that no matter how small the action may appear, it is still necessary. Safety pins appear small in size, however, they are big in what they are DESIGNED to ACHIEVE. A safety pin can hold together things bigger than itself! Your goal or dream may seem small to you, but it holds together your future and the futures of those around you.

Recently, I learned a term called *object permanence*[4]. This term blew my mind. Object permanence is knowing and understanding that "something" is there even though we cannot see it, hear it, smell it, or feel it. This is something we develop as infants, around eight months or so. For instance, have you ever played peek-a-boo with a baby? Babies laugh at this game because when you put your hands up, you suggest you are no longer there. Right when the baby least expects it, you remove your hands from your face and shout "Peek-a-boo!" It's hilarious, because they act so surprised! They really think you left! Like, bruh, all I did was cover my face! I've been here the whole time!

In your spiritual life, have you yet to develop object permanence? Are you in a place where you understand that even though you may not see God working, he is still working? Just as the baby looks for you when your hands cover your face, we sometimes search for God when storms cover our lives. When you didn't get the grade needed to pass that class, the job you applied for, or the husband/wife you wished for, God was still there in the midst of it all.

CREATED TO WIN

So, back to the Power Rangers. Another thing that baffled me about the Power Rangers was they always won! Right when I thought they would be defeated, one of the rangers would throw up their wrists, shout, and a force would come down among their enemies and they would either flee or fall.   The good guys always won. Here's why—the producers of Power Rangers chose the Power Rangers as main characters of the show. The show revolves around them and their "producer-given" purposes. Why would the producer of the show create them with a purpose and not give them everything they needed to be great in that purpose?

Check this out, so because the producer has put so much work into the characters he created, he cannot allow the characters to fail, to do so, would suggest that the producer was unaware of what the characters needed in order to achieve.

Allow me to make it plain. YOU WERE PURPOSED TO WIN! Jeremiah 1:5a (NIV) says, *"Before I formed you in the womb I knew you."* The message of our own Producer is even clearer in Jeremiah 29:11 (NIV) when He says, *"For I know the plans I have for you," declares the LORD, "plans to prosper you and not to harm you, plans to give you hope and a future."*

Trouble is a promotion for promise! Every trial you face, every obstacle placed on your path, every heartache, every disappointment, and every slammed door serves a purpose.

You will not be defeated. You have all the right stuff! Walk confidently in your purpose!

Chapter Three
HATE IS A WEAK EMOTION

Understand this, hate is a weak emotion! Can you imagine wasting so much time and energy on what someone else is doing that you forget your own purpose? Rap artist, Rich Homie Quan makes it clear that our successes, make our haters feel "some type of way"[5].

I had a hard time understanding the "Some Type of Way" emotion. Honestly, at a doctor's office, or in a guidance counselor's office, you will usually see a chart of emotions plastered on the wall. On a scale of one to ten, they ask you to choose the emotion that shows how you feel. Nowhere on that poster will we find the "Some Type of Way" emotion. However, there are a lot of people feeling "some type of way". While Rich Homie Quan may have had a different view on what is considered successful, the point still remains: It is not okay to feel "some type of way" about the successes of others; especially when you have the opportunity to get some success of your own!

YOUR HATERS WILL SEE YOUR PURPOSE, EVEN WHEN YOU CAN'T

In addition to the Power Rangers, Batman was my show! Batman was that guy! Not only did he have the coolest martial arts moves, but Batman was a billionaire and women flocked to him. So it's needless to say that Batman had haters. Batman's only concern was keeping the City of Gotham safe. The death of his parents motivated him to bring judgment upon anyone who caused danger to others. His haters, hated him for this. What if Batman did nothing? What if he just sat around all day and complained about the fact that he lost his parents at such a young age? Would the Joker still have created situations just to bring Batman down? Would the Penguin and Two-Face still have been so adamant about killing him? Would Catwoman still have the same love/hate relationship that she has with him? The answer is no. Batman only had so many haters because his life revealed his purpose.

Check this out. Luke 15:2 (NIV) says, *"But the Pharisees and the teachers of the law muttered, "This man welcomes sinners and eats with them."* First of all, we know who the Pharisees were. They were old school haters. They didn't have Instagram or Facebook, but they used other people to keep a tab on what Jesus was doing. Jesus was out giving sight to the blind, healing the sick, and schooling people on what thus says the Lord. The Pharisees just couldn't get with it. Luke 15:2 tells us these people were so in tune with what Jesus was doing that they knew who he sat with and who he ate with! Back in those times, when someone invited you to eat with them, it was an honor. It's not like now a days when you're offered something to eat, you respond "no" trying to save face and look cute. In those times, if someone asked you to eat with them, you gladly accepted; again it was an honor.

The Pharisees were upset about who Jesus ate with, because they saw it as an honor to eat with him; an honor that sinners did not deserve. But, wait a minute! The Pharisees thought Jesus was a fake, a phony, a magician, they questioned everything he did and refused to believe he was the Messiah. You mean to tell me they were still worried about who had the honor to eat with him?! Can I tell you that your haters can see your greatness more than you can? If Jesus was just some regular Joe on the street, the Pharisees wouldn't have cared who he ate with. But because Jesus did what he was purposed to do, he was the center of the Pharisees' attention, just as Batman was the center of attention for every villain in Gotham City.

Why are our haters angered when they see us walking in our purpose? Well this depends on the type of hater that you are dealing with. Let's review. There are several types of haters. Knowing and identifying them will help you protect your purpose and use their negativity as motivation.

Description	The INSECURE Hater
	This hater can be your best friend, or someone in your inner circle. They once achieved great things, but a few setbacks caused them to become **insecure**. They no longer feel like they have purpose.
	People often compliment them on *"always being real"* or *"keeping it 100"*. But they are not *"real"*, **they are just too insecure to dream**. As a result, they have a *"deep"* and *"prophetic"* negative response for every dream or goal you share with them. The "INSECURE HATER" **never attempts anything outside of their comfort zone.** They are controlled by **a fear of their own greatness**.
	The "INSECURE HATER" always tries to tell you how you feel about them... *before you even say anything.*

Level of Threat to Your Purpose	*Level 1. DANGER, Proceed with caution!* The damage they can inflict *depends upon you.* How much are *you allowing yourself* to take in from them? When they speak to you, does your *mind fabric* begin to say *"I Can't"*? Do you find yourself *agreeing with them more than trying to prove them wrong?* **Beware, this hater will attempt to *talk you OUT of your purpose.***
Dealing with this Hater	Pray for them. Allow their discouraging words to go in one ear and out the other. Understand that it has nothing to do with you. **Most of the time, when people undermine your dreams or predict your doom, they're telling you THEIR story, not YOURS.** Keep walking in your purpose. Maybe they will benefit from hating on you and develop a better perspective about life.
How to Know If YOU Fit the Description	Are you *constantly* **telling others what they can't do, particularly those close to you**? Do you find yourself **discouraging more than encouraging**? Are you **"supposing"** more than you are **supporting**?

Do you find yourself **trying to convince others that they can't do something just because YOU tried and failed**?

Description	**"The Mentee" Hater** We're calling this one "The Mentee" Hater because they hang around you, to be you. *Not to learn from you, but to become YOU! So in this sense, you aren't their friend. You are their "Mentor".* They are always finding ways to show you how your purpose and their purpose are *so much alike*. "The Mentee" Hater has very *little pride* in the beginning. **They do not mind *following you everywhere* or being *known as your protégé or sidekick*.** They're your "Yes" men. **They never tell you when you are wrong, at least not to your face.** "The Mentee" Hater is so hard to spot, because **they *are always there for you*.** They don't mind going the distance. They have ulterior motives. They don't wish to be there because they care about you, it gives them *something to talk about, something to post to social media*. It gives him/her an opportunity to

	spend more time with you and find every hole you thought you covered.
Level of Threat to Your Purpose	**Level 3. Keep Your Eyes Open!!!** Know this—The "Mentee" Hater is an *opportunist* and desires to be better than you. No harm there, right? Wrong. What makes The "Mentee" Hater dangerous is that they don't want to achieve greatness by working their talents, they seek to rob you of your greatness by exposing your weaknesses and pulling those closest to you, to them. The "Mentee" Hater doesn't want what's for them, because they have yet to realize it.
Dealing with this Hater	*Monitor* what you allow The "Mentee" Hater to do with you and for you. Watch the things you say, and the weaknesses you may share with them. The "Mentee" Hater still has growing to do, and that's okay. Continue to help them along their journey, but do it from a far enough distance that you are not burned.

| How to Know If YOU Fit the Description | When you are with your friends, do you find yourself talking about your "mentor" often?   Do you find yourself letting them in on secrets that your "mentor" has shared with you?

 After spending time or doing something with your "mentor", how soon do you take to social media to share your personal experience with the world?

How often do you talk about favors you may have done for your "mentor", or heart to heart conversations the two of you have shared?

Do you desire to have the effect of your "mentor" or the benefits of being your "mentor"? |
|---|---|

| Description | **The Jealous Hater**

This hater can be anybody, even people you really don't know, but majority of the time, The Jealous Hater is a former friend/lover/partner. They hate you because you walked away from the situation with your sanity, and they still feel "some type of way". They never *happen* upon your moves.   They do full blown **RESEARCH** to find out what you are doing.   The Jealous Hater will search through your *Instagram, Facebook, and Twitter* (days, weeks, and even months back) just to find something to **criticize**. |
|---|---|

Level of Threat to Your Purpose	**Level 4. PURPOSE THREATENING!!!** Nothing fuels hate like pain. Hate can sometimes be the residue of a relationship, business, or friendship gone badly. This type of hater is the **most dangerous of all**. They are so wrapped in your purpose, that they have completely forgotten their own. As a matter of fact, the hate for you is so FOR REAL, they will take you down, even if it means taking themselves down in the process. *It's unbelievable, but some people are more concerned with seeing you fail, than seeing themselves achieve.*
Dealing with this Hater	If there is **no way** for you two to reconcile your differences, the best thing to do is **ignore this hater**. Don't give them any attention. Pray that God heals their heart, and helps them to **focus on developing their own purpose instead of trying to destroy yours**.
How to Know If YOU Fit the Description	When someone posts on social media, do you feel like they are talking about you? Do you **scroll** into their posts or do you **search** for them? How many times have you screenshot something related to them just to send to someone else for **negative purposes**?

	Do you find yourself taking credit for **their success**? Do you sometimes feel as though **they don't deserve the success they are achieving?**

Description	**The Relatable Hater** The Relatable Hater finds it easy to **relate** to some aspect of you because they are **family, or they grew up with you**. They feel as though everything you do in life should **RELATE** to them. They hate it when you try to do anything that defines you **OUTSIDE of your RELATION** to them. Example: Auto Mechanics is a traditional work field for my family. However, growing up, I had no desire to work with cars. This made certain family members very upset. They attempted to make me feel "less than a man" because of my decision to go to college and follow my dreams instead of their directions.
Level of Threat to Your Purpose	**Level 2. Stay in touch, but OUT OF REACH!** This hater is so close to home, so close to your heart. They can hurt you **deeper than any other hater**, but you can control the effects of their negativity. The Relatable Hater is upset with you for two reasons. You

	are doing something different and **they feel as though you may "shine" harder than them**, or they feel as though **you may forget them**. You'd think that if anyone had your back, it would be the people that share **the same blood lines** as you. Sad to say, they do have your back….*They have your back at the perfect angle to shove two knives into it.*
Dealing with this Hater	Each time you confront this hater, their argument will be the same. *"Oh, you think you're so much now. Don't forget where you came from! Don't forget who held you down before everybody else! It worked for us, so it can work for you! Don't get beside yourself! "* Take everything this hater says with **a grain of salt**. They really don't matter. Nine times out of ten, the relatable hater is the one with the **least influence in your life** (financially). Remember, just because something worked for *Maw Maw, Paw Paw, and everybody else,* **does not mean that it will work for you. Your purpose can not be mixed up with anybody else's.** The reason most of our families are in the same predicaments they were in *years ago* is because they decided to stick to things that were *relatable*! **Growth and change are not relatable!** Keep doing you!

How to Know If YOU Fit the Description	*As it relates to family members and close friends…* When they changed for the better did it **inspire you** or did you feel like they changed **in spite of you**? Do you feel as though they did certain things to '**show you up**'? Do you encourage them and try to hold them accountable or do you find joy **each time they fall short**? Do you **congratulate** others before you ask why, how, when and where? **Do you compare yourself to them often**? Do you find yourself reminding them of things they used to do? When you make #TBT posts on social media, **do you feel like you are the only one that hadn't changed much**?

WHY ME?!

The pressure from haters can make it hard to breathe. For real! Just knowing that your every move is being scrutinized and criticized is stressful! So take a moment or two and think about your haters from a different point of view. Think about a thief. Before a thief plans his attack, he learns two things. He learns your schedule, and he learns the value of your possessions. The thief has to know that robbing you will be worth the hassle. When have you ever heard a report in which a thief stole something of little value? A thief doesn't go into a house and steal a box of cheerios, he can get that anywhere. He steals items from a particular house, because he knows that is the only way he can get those particular valuables. The fact that your haters chose YOU confirms the value of your purpose.

Your haters strengthen you. Continue to fight their attempts on your purpose! Right now you are the only reason your haters have to wake up in the morning. They love to talk about you. Until they grow into their own purposes, your haters will ALWAYS talk about you. LET THEM! Don't worry about what haters are saying, just focus on what God has said about you! Keep living in your purpose, someone else is depending on it, literally!

We must continue to pray for our haters and learn to forgive their actions. I know, you're probably thinking I'm crazy, but let me explain. My mother is a very sweet woman with a huge heart. As children, she instilled in us the importance of serving and doing right unto others…even those that misuse us. She'd tell us that no matter how bad someone treats us, we should still do our duty in helping them, but instead of feeding them up close, use a long-handled spoon and feed them from a far distance. That's how we must deal with our haters.

As we discussed earlier, our haters are usually people we know or have had close contact with. Using a "long-handled" spoon when dealing with haters allows you to still pray for them and forgive them without having them "too close for comfort". It is okay to stay in touch, but be out of reach!

ADDRESSING THE HATERS

Dear INSECURE Hater,

What happened to you? Where did your dreams go? Do you feel like you may be too old to chase them, or too off track to achieve them? This is not true. Your starting point is NOW! It is time to revamp and renew your ideas. Stop telling others they can't do something just because it didn't work for you. Did you ever take a second and realize that maybe it didn't happen for you because it wasn't meant for you? Maybe the testimony of your failures and where you went wrong will help others to avoid the same mistakes. Continue to share your experience, but do it from a more positive light. When encouraging others, remain positive. You may find just what you need to begin walking in your own purpose again. Best of Luck!

Sincerely,

Mr. /Ms. Tired of Your Negativity

Dear "Mentee" Hater,

Dude, I get it! We all have people that inspire us, many of which we have the privilege of calling a friend. First of all, be grateful for the experiences that you have had with your "mentor". It's a cold world, and finding people you can trust is hard. No, your "mentor" may not have it all together sometimes. If they choose to come to you during those hard times, those experiences shouldn't be shared with others. Understand that God will not bless you by bringing harm to others. No matter how similar your purpose seems to others purposes, they are not the same. You were created to be different! So be different. Be honest with your friend, and let them know where you need help. Everything done in the dark will come to light. Don't allow the lights to pop on and your friend catches you with your hand in their purpose jar! This will ruin the friendship, and you will lose more than you ever gained. GET IT TOGETHER!

Sincerely,

Mr. /Ms. You Can't Help People These Days

Dear Jealous Hater,

Right now, you may feel used, heartbroken, or angry. Sometimes, friendships, relationships, and businesses go sour. At this point, playing the blame game is senseless. They have moved on with their lives. It's time for you to do the same. Take some time and remember the person you fell in love with/became friends with/ decided to go into business with BEFORE things went bad. You need to understand that despite whatever happened, that is still who they are. We all make mistakes, but, people grow! Would you like to be punished for every wrong you've ever done for the rest of your life? Think about the people you may have hurt in your past? How would you feel if you had to deal with their hatred ALL the time? It's time to forgive and do some growing of your own! Don't allow your purpose to die because the relationship/friendship/partnership died. Being jealous takes too much time and energy, let it go! If it was a relationship, you are probably having a hard time letting go because you loved so much about them. Maybe you feel like" They were such a great person, we could be so great together, and oh my gosh, they were created for me…."- Stop right there. They were not created for you, but for their purpose, just as you were created for your own. So many times, we feel as though just because someone is a good person that makes them a good person for us. This is not always the case. Learn to appreciate people for who they are, and not who they could be to you. So if the relationship goes bad, you don't feel like they walked away with a part of you. Your future is calling you, but you can't answer because your lines are tied up with someone who has already hung up the phone! Once you begin letting some things go, the right connections will happen and make others who walked away a thing of the past! Do you for you, boo!

Sincerely,

Mr. /Ms. Let Me Live

Dear Relatable Hater,

Ain't nobody trying to forget you or outshine you! We will never forget who we are or where we came from because it MADE US WHO WE ARE TODAY. However, it does not define who we will be tomorrow! We don't attempt to do better just to make you look bad, we attempt to do better because WE want to do better. Just because our dreams may not align, does not mean our hearts can't. The love we have for you, will be there no matter what. You still have purpose too! Instead of being jealous-hearted, ask for advice on how you can make your own dreams happen! I know you have dreams deep down inside. Tap into those dreams and make them a reality. Somewhere along the way, we took a step back and realized that we wanted to do something different. Accept that. Just because we do not want to be a part of the family business or traditions does not mean that we don't respect it or appreciate it. Are you sure that you even like the family business or traditions? Misery loves company. Sometimes, we subconsciously pull others into the same situations we are in, because we are afraid to be in them alone. This is not fair. Again, think about your dreams and aspirations. What would you have done differently if you had someone to push you towards them? It's not too late to start supporting those around you who have decided to do things differently. Come on now!

Sincerely,

Mr. /Ms. Can I Be Great

If you fit any of the hater descriptions we discussed, don't feel "some type of way". Just remember to put so much effort into bettering YOURSELF that you don't even have time to focus on anyone else, especially in a negative way. Hate is a weak emotion because it allows you to take the window seat on someone else's ride! It is so easy to give directions from the passenger or back seat! Have you ever been on a road trip with people that criticized you for getting lost, but once they got behind the wheel, they did the exact same! It is easy to view where other people fall short or make the wrong turns, but when the views change and require different lenses to see clearly, it is not so easy to point out the mistakes. **Stop looking for window seats and start searching for mirrors.** Get yourself together. You will never know the greatness that lies within if you are so busy tracking the greatness of other people. You are not in competition with anyone but yourself! Plan to outdo your past, not other people.

Chapter Four
GETTING A HANDLE ON YOUR
EMOTIONS

Have you ever had an argument or discussion with someone who seemed okay at first; they were responsive, smiling, and calm but suddenly began to cry, holler, smack their hands, have panic attacks, and blow bubbles all at the same time? Okay, maybe it wasn't THAT bad, but they went from 0 to 100 so fast that it confused the heck out of you! If you're anything like me, you probably got up and quietly (but quickly) walked away. Or, maybe (just maybe) the dramatic person, was YOU and you just sat there wondering why the other person left you, why they couldn't understand you. Bruh, because you're CRAZY! That's why. No, seriously, it's confusing to understand why we are sometimes able to display so many emotions at once. What sets us off? What causes this emotional instability? There's no one answer to this.

Disclaimer: I'm no psychologist. If you are experiencing any type of emotional instability, go get help, QUICK! There are many people in our high schools, communities, churches, hospitals, and even colleges and universities that are skilled in helping people in this area. Go talk to a professional. In the meantime, let's take a look into some of the things that may trigger emotional instability and how we can best deal with them.

LOOSE SCREWS

Let's take a moment and think about an unstable chair. A chair can be unstable for several reasons. One of the main reasons is that it can simply have a couple of loose screws. As a child, I often heard adults say "Be still in that chair before you mess it up. If you're gonna do all that wiggling and moving, you might as well sit on the floor!" I'm like, bruh, chill! How am I gonna mess this chair up just by moving around in it? As I got older, I understood that the purpose of the chair, was to support you as you sit in it, not wiggle in it, not stand on it to reach something, and not to use as a desk or whatever other things we may use chairs for from time to time.

Anything done in the chair outside of its purpose has the potential to loosen the screws and make the chair unstable for sitting. Now think about your mind in the same aspect. What have you been allowing to wiggle and move about in your mind? What has loosened your mental screws? What have you allowed to make your mind so unstable that it can no longer support your purpose?

Today, many adults are unstable because of things that happened during their childhood. As children, we have no control of the things that happen to us, yet we are greatly affected by them once we reach adulthood. Frederick Douglass once said "It is easier to build strong children than to repair broken men." When I heard this quote, I was like, dang. That's real. Douglass's statement gives us insight into why there are so many adults with child-like mentalities. His statement serves as a forewarning for adults that either have children or influence children, but what does it say to adults that are already broken because of situations that occurred when WE were children? How do we go about recovering from a damaging childhood? How do we erase the memories of staying with a tyrant/grandma while mama worked 2-3 jobs to provide? How do we erase the confusion of not ever understanding why…Why we were treated differently than other grandchildren? Why we were never good enough for her love, care, and affection? How do we rid our minds of the harsh verbal abuse? How do we heal our bodies of the physical pain and turmoil?

My grandmother passed away almost ten years ago, but I can still feel the sting of the way she made me feel. I can still hear her shouting "You ain't s$%!! You will never make it to see 18. You will never graduate from high school! You will never amount to anything!" She always singled me out, and teased me. She would keep me up, making me clean at strange times in the night. The treatment was horrible. So many times, I ran away from home to escape the abuse and most importantly, to get a peace of mind. It is impossible to build up a child in a place where their mind cannot grow.

I never really understood the impact my grandmother made until I was in college, trying to pass the Praxis Exam. All educators must take the Praxis in order to be certified as a highly-qualified teacher. Well I'd taken this test 4 times, failing each test by only a few points. Once, I was literally one point away. They rescored it and I still failed! Talk about being mad—I was furious! In addition to failing the test, I was dealing with a toxic relationship, other family issues, and trying to maintain my household. From the back of my mind, my grandma's words began to creep into my thoughts. Immediately, I was a child in her home again. I heard her words so vividly; it was as if she was standing right behind me.

I went to my other grandmother, Grandma Jackie. She began

to speak over me. "If He brought you to it, He will bring you through it." she proclaimed. "Now go and do great things." With that, she placed $100 dollars in my hand. Okay, Grandma Jackie! She had no idea of the deposit she had made into my life. I'm not talking about the money. It was a blessing, but the greatest deposit was emotional. Her words gave me the strength to overcome the "I can't" mindset that began to settle in during that moment of despair. One month later, I passed the Praxis and now I teach. TURN UP!

TAKING OUT THE TRASH

There is so much power in words and actions. People can apologize for things they may have said or done to hurt us, but as humans we will never forget what once caused us pain. We can try with all our might, but we will never fully rid our minds of those thoughts or feelings. So where does it all go? What happens to those thoughts and feelings? Well, you know how trash that is piled up for a while begins to smell? The same thing happens to our feelings or thoughts of pain. Sometimes that stuff piles up in our minds for so long that it begins to STINK. Soon after, our attitudes begin to stink because our attitudes are direct reflections of what is going on in our minds and in our hearts. For a lot of us, it is time to take out the trash!

When garbage men take our trash, the trash is sorted through and taken to the appropriate site. Some of the trash is sent to a decomposing site, where overtime, it will decompose or break down. The other trash is taken to a recycling site. When we recycle, we take trash that cannot decompose and turn it into something useful. You cannot decompose hurt and pain, but you can recycle it! The bible tells us that all things work together for our good.

In chapter 3, we discussed haters and how we should allow their actions to push our purpose, and not paralyze our purpose. My grandma could have been right about me, but because I allowed my mind to recycle the negative words she spoke into me, I was able to prove her wrong. Recycle the hurt and the pain others may have caused. Use their hurtful actions as a reminder to keep going. Use them as a reminder to get up every morning and keep striving to be great. Know that your story does not end or begin in the negative words others may have spoken over your life, but in the purpose in which you were created.

You are not worthless. You are not too messed up for someone to love you. You are not dumb. You are not ugly. You are not too dark. You are not too fat. Your scars are not hideous. You are not a failure. Whatever negativity that has been spoken over you, release it now! Hold your head up, YOU ARE AWESOME!

DYSFUNCTIONAL RELATIONSHIPS

While it is true, most of our emotional instability may be due to things inflicted upon us, a lot of it is due directly to relationships we allow to hold us captive. Relationships now a days can be so confusing. With phrases like, "situationship" "we just chilling" "friends with benefits" and "that's bae" stemming about, it's no wonder that so many people are unstable because of relationships.

First and foremost, let's look at the word relationship. Relationship means connection. The word can be used to describe the connection between two people, ex: students and teachers (student-teacher relationship) OR mother and daughter (mother-daughter relationship). The key word here is connection. In order for there to be a connection, there has to be 2 separate ends or two people to connect. If your charger is connected to your phone, but not to an outlet, can the charger still serve its purpose? Oh okay then! That alone should have set a lot of you free, but just in case it didn't, I'll make it plain. In order for a relationship to serve its purpose, BOTH people have to be connected.

A lot of people are in relationships, by themselves. They are talking to themselves, arguing with themselves, cooking for two by themselves, with someone else present the entire time. Can I tell you that this is enough to make anybody crazy?! So if you consider yourself to be in a "relationship" with anybody, you need to first check the connection.

If you have Facebook friends that are anything like mine, you know that Facebook can be a hilarious source of entertainment. Especially Facebook posts like these:

Saturday: 12:45 a.m. **Tequila LovingRayRayAlways Jenkins** is Out wit da bae! We finna tUrNuP!!!

Saturday 1:50 a.m **Tequila IdontNeedNobodyButMe Jenkins** FORGET these _____! Imma iNdEpEnDeNt woman Boo-Boo! Me Myself and I, It's Tequila _____!!!

Saturday 3:00a.m. **Tequila SoHurtAndConfused Jenkins** Missing the bae!!!! #him #us #ineedthat

Saturday 3:45a.m. **Tequila StillMs.RayRay Jenkins** We gone show the world!! I love bae! We forever! #know that!

Y'ALL this is crazy!! While these are not authentic postings, they are very similar to the posts we often see on social media. They are but reflections of what is actually going on in the minds of so many dysfunctional people. It's hard not to be dysfunctional with hits out like "All of Me" by John Legend. Don't get me wrong, the song is nice. I'm a huge John Legend fan, but some of the messages that the song sends makes so many people feel as though dysfunction is okay.

"What's going on in that beautiful mind, I'm on your magical mystery ride, and I'm so dizzy, don't know what hit me, but I'll be alright." –Excerpt from "All of Me"[6] *by John Legend*

Okay I get it, when you really love someone, you accept it all. No, every day won't be sunny, you take the good with the bad. I get that, but come on! I don't know about you, but I don't want to be on ANYONE's magical mystery ride, being dizzy is not fun and neither is being hit. It is songs like this and other things in our environment that make us feel like Tequila and believe that dysfunction is love.

Even dysfunctional friendships are unhealthy. Have you ever had a friend that was cool with you one day, and the next they were upset with you about something petty, something you never even noticed? Instead of talking about it, they got upset, made Instagram posts, but never came to you about the issue. Can I tell you this is not a friend? If you call them a "friend", you need to find a new term of "endearment" for them.

Dysfunctional relationships wear on your mind because they cause you to think in a dysfunctional manner. You become indecisive in your choice making and defensive with other people who have absolutely nothing to do with your relationship. Being in a dysfunctional relationship hinders your purpose. It takes your focus away from where it really needs to be! No relationship is worth your sanity or your peace of mind. Relationships should better you and build you, not have your "head under water". We have so many battles to face on a day to day basis to keep our purposes alive. Why should we add on to that by connecting to people who bring dysfunction into our lives?

Relationships and friendships are choices that we make. No one can MAKE you be with them, or be their friend. So today, take a look at your friendships and relationships. Are any of them unhealthy? Have you just been stringing things along because the two of you "have history"? Having "history" does not mean you will or should have a future! If any relationship or friendship brings you more heartache than happiness, do yourself a favor and start feeding those people with long handled spoons.

When learning to ride a bike we are taught that when we fall off we should "get up, dust off, and try again." While this is a great mindset to have in several aspects of life, when it comes to relationships, we should not. This is one of the main reasons for so many dysfunctional relationships. You have people in new relationships dealing with old feelings. That's just like mixing a new quart of milk with spoiled milk and expecting it to taste fresh. Instead of being so quick to jump back into relationships, or reconnect with new people, you should first take a moment and reevaluate yourself. Spend some time working on you and your emotional bank account.

I'm sure most of you have a checking and/or savings account with a bank. Accounts are set up so that you can make monetary withdrawals and deposits. If there are deposits made to an account there will be growth in that account, however, if you withdraw more than you deposit you run into a term called insufficient funds. A lot of us are stuck in the area of insufficiencies as it relates to our emotions. We have been unable to make deposits based on what has happened in our past experiences. As unfortunate as this may seem, some people would prefer to stay in the area of insufficiencies. When your mind is plagued with doubt, frustration, and guilt, it is probable that you won't achieve. For some this is comfortable; the dysfunction and the emotional instability doesn't bother them at all. For you, this is not the case.

You were created to WIN! Philippians 4:13 say, *"I can do all things through Christ who strengthens me."* Did you notice the word "all" All is a small three letter word but it leaves out nothing. All is included in all! So the first step to making deposits into your emotional bank account is telling yourself what you can do, then do it!

GETTING REVENGE IS NOT YOUR JOB

So many times, after we are done wrong, we instantly want that sweet taste of revenge. I'm sure many of you have heard the statement, "When you dig one grave, you better dig two." It doesn't matter what the situation is, you should under no circumstances try to "get someone back" for what they did to you.

Do you remember back in elementary school you'd be sitting in class, minding your own business and someone would throw something across the room and hit you? After finding out who it was, you'd sit and plan the perfect plan of attack. You'd wait all day long and right when you thought the teacher wasn't looking you started to launch the attack! As soon as the object leaves your fingertips, the teacher turns around and you'd get in trouble. Vengeance belongs to our Father, not us. When we try to avenge ourselves, we end up getting into more trouble and loosening more screws than were loose in the first place.

It is important that we forgive. We must ask God to forgive those that hurt us. We must ask him to show them where they hurt us, and pray that he fixes their hearts before they go on to hurt other people. We have to love people (not just the people we like) with the love of Christ. Christ loves us when we don't even love ourselves. Even when are so connected with the world that we lose our connection with him, he still loves us. It is this same unconditional love in which we should love those we've let go. Forgive them. Not just for them, but for yourself. It happened. Now let it go.

Back in 2005, I went home to visit, and decided to go see my grandmother. I was tired of carrying the burden and had made a decision to forgive her of all she had done. I was ready to let it go. Before leaving, I even told her that I loved her. At the time, my grandmother was no longer able to speak, so she simply nodded her head and smiled. Later on in the day, just as I was heading back to AAMU, I got a phone call that my grandmother had passed away.

I often think, what if I didn't forgive her? What if I just passed up the opportunity to go by the hospital that day in 2005? I would have become everything that I hated about my grandma. Well, you may be asking, Chris, what should I do if I never got the opportunity to forgive? What if the person I need to forgive has passed away or is out of reach? Still forgive them. Forgive them with your heart. Set yourself free. The sooner you do it, the better. It doesn't matter if it was a mother who abandoned you, a husband that walked out, or a friend that didn't remain true; you still need to forgive them. You will never be able to fully walk in your purpose until you do.

Chapter Five

TRAIN HARD, GROW STRONG

Recently, I had a conversation with Christion (my 5 year old nephew) that blew my mind.

"What's up, Fat?" I said.

"What's up?" he responded like usual.

"What do you want to be when you grow up?"

"I want to be a police officer...and I want to be grown."

After discussing why he wanted to be a police officer, he began to explain why he wanted to be "grown".

"Uncle Chris, I don't want nobody telling me what to do." He explained.

"Fat, I'm 30 years old, and your grandma still tells me what to do, because I'm her child." I replied, *"She'll always be able to tell me what to do."*

"Yea, well, that's different Uncle Chris. It's not the same."

I was blown! He didn't even know the capacity of what he said! It's not the same! When I was a teenager, I would always shout about how I could not wait to get out of the house! Like most teenagers (and 5-year-olds obviously), being told what to do got on my nerves! I saw my mother's direction as a bad thing. Now, in adulthood, I understand that all the fussing had a purpose. It served as training to prepare me to move into the world on my own.

My nephew was right, it is different. 1 Corinthians 13:11 (NIV) says *"When I was a child, I talked like a child, I thought like a child, I reasoned like a child. When I became a man, I put the ways of childhood behind me."* As a child, I despised direction. Now that I'm "grown" my mother's direction no longer bothers me because I am mature enough to understand the necessity of training.

Today, so many "grown" adults are living on their own with the same childish mentality they had as teenagers living with their parents. They still despise training. They fail to realize that training is necessary for growth.

We use TRAINING wheels until we are able to ride a bike without them.

Before becoming active in the military, you must go through basic TRAINING.

When starting a new job, you have to go through new hire TRAINING.

Children go through potty TRAINING to learn how to "go" on their own.

As you can see, our life consists of much training. Let's go deeper and actually look at the word training.

Training[7]: root word: train

Train (noun): 1. Mode of transportation. (He rode the train from Birmingham to New Orleans.)

2. Extended part of a gown that trails or follows behind. (The bride's train was really long!)

3. A process used to produce a certain result. (He had to train really hard to become a policeman.)

Most of the time, when we look at the definition of a word, we see several definitions that don't really mean anything to us. Like dang Webster, I only needed one! This situation is different. Take a look at each definition of the word train. Each definition gives us insight on how we should view training as it relates to growth. In order for us to be transported to our next destination in life, we must go through a process of growth. What we learn in this process shouldn't stop when the training is over, however, just as a bride's train follows her down the aisle into a new life, our training should follow us wherever we go.

Our life training doesn't always come in the form of new hire training, basic training or potty training. Sometimes, training may come through having your heart broken, losing a loved one, failing a class, or being fired from a job. I'm sure you've heard the saying "It's not what you go through, it's how you respond to it." Well, it's through these situations that we get the exposure needed to learn how to respond to life maturely.

EXPOSURE

At age one, my nephew, Cameron, was fascinated with fire. We were constantly telling him, "Don't touch the stove, its hot," "Don't stand by the grill that fire will get you," and "That iron will burn you!" One day, we were in the kitchen and as usual he was warned several times to stay away from the hot stove. As I opened the stove to take out the baked chicken, he moved in to touch the stove. We all know what happened next. AHHHHH!!!! He hollered so loudly! He cried so much that he literally left a small spill of tears on the floor. After we got him cleaned up, we further explained to him the dangers of hot things. To this day, he thinks twice before approaching hot things. What am I saying? Until we are exposed to certain things we don't desire to change. Honestly, until exposure happens, we are not even aware that we should change.

I sometimes wondered why so many young people get too college and GET LOOSE! I mean they turn up every day, go to every party, club, etc. I realized the reason they are so "buck wild", is because many of them have never been exposed to such freedom. Growth exposes us to things to improve our responses in life. Just as new college students sometimes have no idea how to respond to such freedom, many of us have no idea as to how to respond to certain life situations, because we have never been exposed to them. After we are exposed to them, we handle them in a different way. For instance, your first check. The first time you got a check (WITH YOUR NAME ON IT) you probably went HAM! I mean, yeah, before that, you've had money before, but a check made out to you?!

Whether it was a refund check or from your first job, you didn't know how to act! You probably brought things you didn't need, splurged on people who wouldn't have spent a dime on you, and ate out every single day. Shortly after (maybe a day or two later), you were broke and realized that it would be a while before you got another check. In that moment, you learned a valuable lesson about saving. At this point in your life (I hope), because you were exposed to #thestruggle, you are a bit more mindful of your spending habits.

GET OVER IT?!

Have you ever been "going through the motions" and someone you talk to tells you to just "get over it"? I have. I always thought this was the realest advice EVER. Man, just get over it! It's that simple!

"I just lost my job." You'll be fine, but you have to get over it!

"Girl, I just found out he cheated on me." So what girl, we 'bout to turn up! Get over it!

"Bruh, she's been seeing another guy." Man, forget that chick, get over it!

"I'm gonna have to retake this class next year." Dude, it'll be okay. Get over it!

"I didn't make the basketball team this year." It's all good, maybe next year! Just get over it.

Get over it is the worst advice anyone can ever give you! As a matter of fact, it's the reason there are many people in their

30's and 40's still acting and responding to situations as if they are 21. Have you ever seen (while watching sports) athletes jump for whatever reason and land wrong? If you're an athlete, I know you just flinched at the thought. When this happens, athletes sometimes sprain an ankle or hurt themselves in some way. Can I tell you that sometimes we have not grown enough (spiritually) to jump over things? Where we are in life often requires us to go through instead of getting over. Sometimes when we jump over things, what meets us when we land is more painful than the obstacle we were trying to get over in the first place.

In track, there's an event called hurdling. Hurdling consists of running and jumping over barriers called hurdles. Picture this. A runner is practicing hurdling and plans to run the track three times. If he successfully jumps over the hurdle, when he circles the track again, the hurdle will still be there. In track, this is a good thing. In your life, it is not. If you continue to jump over your hurdles they will only continue to meet you again. I often think of the words of my Grandma Jackie, "If God brought you to it, he will bring you through it." THROUGH IT, not over it, not around it, not under it, but through it! On the other side of pain, is purpose.

God brings us to different situations so that when we are done going through it, we emerge on the other side stronger and more purposeful. When you get through it, you allow yourself to internalize the situation completely. You are able to realize what hurt, why it hurt, and how you will prevent it from hurting you again. When you get over it, you run into the same situations because you never learned the lesson when training was in session the first time.

Here's another thing about hurdles. Hurdles are set at measured HEIGHTS and DISTANCES depending upon the event. When training is in session, we sometimes miss the lesson because we are so busy worried about why other people's "hurdles" don't seem to be affecting them as much as our own are affecting us. We have to remember that unlike sports, we are not in competition with anyone. Your life obstacles are measured at the HEIGHT and DISTANCE in which you need to grow. Your purpose, is not their purpose. Get YOUR training. Stay in YOUR lane. Run YOUR race.

Going through your hurdles may be uncomfortable. It's training. It's not meant to be comfortable. When something is comfortable. It is relatable. It's the norm. You are familiar with it. As we discussed in Chapter 3, growing is not meant to be relatable. Training takes you outside of your comfort zone and releases you into your purpose.

RE-POT. RE-PLANT. RE-SOIL.

When I was in elementary school, we had a class plant. One day, my teacher took the plant out of one pot and put it in another one. This completely confused me. I was like, YO, what is she doing? That makes no sense. Here's what I didn't realize. The new pot, was bigger. And it had to be. You see the majority of a plant's growth happens within its roots. If the roots no longer have space to grow, the plant will not grow. So when a plant reaches a certain size it has to be taken out of the smaller flower pot and put into a bigger one, so that the roots have space to grow. Another thing that baffled me, was she didn't use the old soil to re-pot the plant. She put new soil in the new pot with the old plant. Soil holds the nutrients that plants need to grow. The old soil was no good because the plant had already gotten all the nutrients it needed from that soil in the old pot. Have you out grown your "flower pot"? In other words, are you still trying to grow in a situation that is stunting your growth? Are you taking old soil into new pots? Some of us are being taken OUT of situations that we can no longer grow in. When you are removed from places in which you can no longer grow, be careful of what you decide to take with you. Some of the things and people you desire to bring along have lost their nutrients. They have lost their purpose in your life.

As children, we wanted to wear our parent's clothes or shoes. When we tried them on, they just didn't fit right. They were too big. We needed to do a bit more growing. Right now your goals and dreams may not fit you because you have yet to grow and mature in to a place where you can walk in them. When we mature, we grow to the place where we can receive and achieve our goals and dreams.

Think of how many times you've asked God for something. God may not have given it to you right at the moment, but he gave it to you right when you needed it. What if God had given you just what you needed at the wrong time? Would you have been able to appreciate it as much as you do now? Would you have still used it for the purpose it was intended? Would you have been mature enough to handle it or would you have forgotten God because you were not in a place where you could handle the distraction and still maintain your relationship with him? Sometimes God's slow response isn't a no. It could simply mean, not right now.

Growth and maturity come after we make the decision to do so. When we are convicted to change we begin to grow up and become a better us. Without this conviction, we waste time in a childish mindset.

I CAN'T IS FOR BROKE FOLKS!

Are you ready to see your purpose? Has it been like a baby, growing inside of you, kicking and squirming, ready to be released? Well take a deep breath and PUSH! Push through life's ups and downs! Push through your emotions! Push through your training! Push through your haters! Push through your own desires and GET THAT BABY OUT OF THERE! The mind is a place in which we all struggle. Sometimes, we may have what I like to call, "The R. Kelly psychosis", (my mind is telling me NOOOO!) It is good to listen to our minds sometimes (like in our "R. Kelly" moments), but when our mind is telling us NO when it relates to our dreams and purposes, we need to take a second and remind ourselves that we can do ALL things; nothing is impossible!

If Nelson Mandela can become president at 80, if 50 Cent got shot nine times and still made a record, if men in their 70s and 80s are still having babies, then it's not too late or too hard for you to fulfill your own dreams! Sit at the feet of your problems and work out every insecurity. Pray, meditate, cry, and forgive! Walk in favor, faith, and confidence. Clear your head of EVERY "can't" because I can't is for broke folks!

ACKNOWLEDGEMENTS

All glory, praise and honor to God for using me and giving me the vision for this book

To my mom, Candis Martin, for believing in me and pushing me to not only be a better person, but a better man. I love you dearly.

To my dad, Arthur Sands, for impacting my life in a major way. Love you dad.

To my sister, Christina Peak, for keeping me on my toes. I love you dearly.

To my niece and nephews, Serenity, Christion, and Cameron, for pushing me and reminding me to live what I preach. Love you all with all of my heart.

To my best friend/my brother, Pastor Adrian Davis, what can I say! Words alone cannot express the depths of my heart as it pertains to how I feel in our friendship. Thank you for being here, pushing me to grow & challenging me to go forth in my purpose for the last 14 years.

To my family, Grandma Jackie, Uncle Bruce, Aunt Geraldine, Granny Money, Bruce Jr. Nate, Aunt Robin, Caylen, Alexis, Brandon, Kim, Wesley, and everyone else. Thank you for believing in me.

To my friends, Kiatra Jones, Jamall Black, Zena Buckley, Sarah Lane, Karla Jones Clark, Kendeil Verrett, Bruce Burks, Jamaal Black, Keith Haynes, Bobby Oats, Brenton Martin, Brittany Morton, Steven Green, LaBoris Cole, & Jennifer Payne thank you all for the push! When I wanted to give up your words, presence, or texts really helped me. I'm truly grateful for friends like you all!

To Keen Vision Editing, LLC for helping me in pushing out this "baby"! Thanks for everything!

To Pastor Jason and First Lady Barbara Scales thank you for seeing greatness in me even when I didn't always see it in myself. Thank you for allowing me to be me and work with some Phenomenal Teens (SWAGG MINISTRY) I LOVE YOU ALL!!! I am blessed to be a member of a PHENOMENAL church, BELIEVERS FAITH FELLOWSHIP! THANK YOU!

To Pastor T.C. Johnson, thank you for helping to mold me from a boy to a man. Thank you for believing in my gifts and sharing it with everyone, especially St. Luke, love you.

To Coach Stanley Jackson, I literally don't have enough room to show my appreciation for how you've impacted my life. As I sit trying to type this, tears are literally flowing from my eyes. You have been one of my role models since I was a big-head, skinny body in your 6th grade health class. You were there to watch me grow up and you are still here. Thank you! Thank you! Thank you!

JOURNALING WITH CHRIS

Journaling is not only therapeutic, but it is an awesome way to assess what you've learned and apply it to everyday living. For one week, challenge yourself to journal for at least 30 minutes a day. Turn off your phone! Go somewhere quiet and distraction-free. Don't rush through it. Take your time to journal about each question!

Day 1: What are something's you need to let go?

Day 2: What would you do if time and resources were not an issue?

Day 3: What is one positive habit you would like to add to your life? What is one negative habit that you would like to stop?

Day 4: What are some I CAN statements that you will add to your daily walk?

Day 5: List all of your long term and short term goals. What steps will you take to achieve each one?

Day 6: Who makes up your support team? List ways in which you hold each other accountable.

Day 7: Do you have any dreams or desires that seem out of reach? What's blocking you from achieving? How can you tear down the barriers keeping you away from your dreams/desires?

THE "I CAN" AGREEMENT

I, _____, agree to make the proper steps to change my mind and my world. I will protect my mind fabric. I will no longer use the word "can't". I believe in my dreams. I will work hard to achieve my goals. I will not give up on my purpose. My haters will not stop me. My past will no longer slow me down. I release everything that stunts my growth. I will accept training. I will love, forgive, and encourage others, more importantly, I will love, forgive, and encourage myself. I am ready, willing, and able to walk in my purpose!!!!

X
_____
Signature

CITATIONS

Chapter 1
1. "conditioning." Webster, Merriam, 2014. July 2014.

2. Future. 2011. *Squares Out Your Circle.* Ft. Rocko.

Chapter 2
3. Wasserman, R. (1994). Go Go Power Rangers [On Album Mighty Morphin Power Rangers The Album: A Rock Adventure]. Saban Records.

4. Cherry, K. 2014. "What Is Object Permanence?" <http://psychology.about.com/od/oindex/g/object-permanence.htm>.

Chapter 3
5. Quan, Rich Homie. 2013. Type of Way. Comp. Yung Carter Dequantes Lamar.

Chapter 4
6. Legend, John. 2013. *All of Me.* Comp. Toby Gad, Dave Tozer, John Stephens.

Chapter 5
7. "training." Webster, Merriam, 2014. July 2014.

CONTACT CHRIS

To share your #ICan Story with Chris, to order merchandise, or to invite Chris to your next event, you may contact him the following ways:

Via email at:

Chriscsands@gmail.com

Facebook:

ChrisSandsSpeaks

Twitter:

@CSands8

Instagram:

@chrissandsspeaks

You may also visit Chris' website at:

www.chrissandsspeaks.org

You may also contact *Covenant Brothers Publishing* via email at:

CovenantBrothersPub@gmail.com

Made in the USA
Columbia, SC
08 January 2025

49374748R00037